THE SECRET OF THE
CROSS

THE SECRET OF THE
CROSS

Andrew Murray

PUBLICATIONS

Fort Washington, PA 19034

The Secret of the Cross
Published by CLC Publications

U.S.A.
P.O. Box 1449, Fort Washington, PA 19034

UNITED KINGDOM
CLC International (UK)
Unit 5, Glendale Avenue, Sandycroft, Flintshire, CH5 2QP

ISBN (paperback): 978-1-61958-296-5
ISBN (e-book): 978-1-61958-297-2

Unless otherwise noted, all Scripture quotations are from the Holy Bible, New King James Version, copyright © 1979, 1980, 1982 by Thomas Nelson, Inc. Used by permission. All rights reserved.

Italics in Scripture quotations are the emphasis of the author.

Cover design by Mitch Bolton.

Introduction

THE question often arises: How is it, with so much churchgoing, Bible reading, and prayer, that a Christian can fail to live a life of complete victory over sin and will lack the love and joy of the Lord? One of the most important answers, undoubtedly, is that he does not know what it is to die to himself and to the world. Yet without this, God's love and holiness cannot have their dwelling place in his heart. He has repented of some sins, but knows not what it is to turn, not only from sin, but from his old nature and self-will.

Yet this is what the Lord Jesus taught. He said to the disciples that if any man would come after Him, he must hate and lose his own life. He taught them to take up the cross. That meant they were to consider their life as sinful and under sentence of death. They must give up themselves, their own will and power, and any goodness of their own. When their Lord had died on the cross, they would then learn what it was to die to themselves and the world, and to live their life in the fullness of God.

Our Lord used the apostle Paul to put this still more clearly. Paul never knew Christ after the flesh. Through the Holy Spirit, however, Christ was revealed in his heart, and he could testify: "I have been crucified with Christ; it is no longer I who live, but Christ lives in me" (Gal. 2:20). In more than one of his epistles the truth is made clear that we are dead to sin, with Christ, and receive and experience the power of a new life through the continual working of God's Spirit in us each day.

As the season of Lent approaches each year, our thoughts become occupied with the sufferings and death of our Lord. Emphasis will be laid, in the preaching, on Christ dying for us on the cross as the foundation of our salvation. Less is said about our death *with* Christ. The subject is a deep and difficult one, yet every Christian needs to consider it. It is my earnest desire to help those Christians who are considering this great truth: that death to self and to the world is necessary for a life in the love and joy of Christ.

I have sought to explain the chief words of our Lord and of His disciples on this subject. May I point out two things to my reader. First, take time to read over what you do not understand at once. Spiritual truth is not easy to grasp. But experience has taught me that God's words, taken into the heart and meditated on with prayer, help the soul by degrees to understand the truth. And second, be assured that only through the continual teaching of the Holy Spirit in your heart will you be able to appropriate spiritual truths. The great work of the Holy Spirit is to reveal Christ in our hearts and lives as the Crucified One who dwells within us. Let this be the chief aim of all your devotion: complete dependence on God, and an expectation of continually receiving all goodness and salvation from Him alone. Thus will you learn to die to yourself and to the world, and be kept through the continual working of the Holy Spirit.

Let us pray fervently for each other that God may teach us what it is to die with Christ—a death to ourselves and to the world; a life in Christ Jesus.

Your servant in the Lord,
ANDREW MURRAY

Prayer

Heavenly Father, how can I adequately thank You for the unspeakable gift of Your Son on the cross! How can I thank You for eternal salvation, wrought out by that death on the cross! Jesus died for me that I might live eternally. Through His death on the cross I am dead to sin and live in the power of His life.

Father in heaven, teach me, I humbly entreat You, what it means that I am dead with Christ and can live my life in Him. Teach me to realize that my sinful flesh is wholly corrupt and nailed to the cross to be destroyed, that the life of Christ may be manifest in me.

Teach me, above all, to believe that I cannot either understand or experience this except through the continual working of the Holy Spirit dwelling within me. Father, for Christ's sake I ask it.

AMEN.

"Jesus hath now many lovers of His heavenly kingdom, but few bearers of His cross. He hath many desirous of consolation, but few of tribulation. He findeth many companions of His table, but few of His abstinence. All desire to rejoice with Him, few are willing to endure anything for Him, or with Him. Many follow Jesus unto the breaking of bread, but few to the drinking of the cup of His passion. Many reverence His miracles, few follow the ignominy of His cross."

THOMAS A KEMPIS

The Redemption of the Cross

*Christ has redeemed us from the curse of
the law, having become a curse for us.*

Galatians 3:13

SCRIPTURE teaches us that there are two points of view from which we may regard Christ's death upon the cross. The one is the *redemption of the cross*: Christ dying for us as our complete deliverance from the curse of sin. The other, the *fellowship of the cross*: Christ taking us up to die with Him and making us partakers of the fellowship of His death in our own experience.

In our text we have three great, unsearchable thoughts. The law of God has pronounced a curse on all sin and on all that is sinful. Christ took our curse upon Him—yea, became a curse—and so destroyed its power, and in that cross we now have everlasting redemption from sin and all its power. The cross reveals to us man's sin as *under* the curse, Christ *becoming* a curse and so *overcoming* it, and our full and everlasting deliverance *from* the curse.

In these thoughts the lost and most hopeless sinner finds a sure ground for confidence and hope. God had indeed in Paradise pronounced a curse upon this earth and all that belongs to it. On Mount Ebal, in connection with the public reading of the law, half of the people of Israel were twelve times over to pronounce a curse on all sin (see Deut. 27:13–26). In addition, there would be in their midst a continual reminder of it: "He who is hanged is acccursed of God" (21:23). And yet who could ever have thought that the Son of God Himself would die upon the accursed tree, and become a curse for us? But such is in very deed the gospel of God's love, and the penitent sinner can now rejoice in the confident assurance that the curse is forever put away from all who believe in Christ Jesus.

The preaching of the redemption of the cross is the foundation and center of the salvation the gospel brings us. To those who believe its full truth it is a cause of unceasing thanksgiving. It gives us boldness to rejoice in God. There is nothing which will keep the heart more tender toward God, enabling us to live in His love and to make Him known to those who have never yet found Him. God be praised for the redemption of the cross!

The Fellowship of the Cross

Let this mind be in you which was also in Christ Jesus.
Philippians 2:5

PAUL here tells us what that mind was in Christ: He emptied Himself; He took the form of a servant; He humbled Himself, even to the death of the cross. It is this mind that was in *Christ*—the deep humility in which He gave up His life to the very death—that is to be the spirit that animates *us*. It is thus that we shall prove and enjoy the blessed fellowship of His cross.

Paul had said (2:1), "If there is any *consolation* in Christ,"—the Comforter was come to reveal His real presence in them—"if any *fellowship* of the Spirit,"—it was in this power of the Spirit that they were to breathe the spirit of the crucified Christ and manifest His disposition in the fellowship of the cross in their lives. Consolation and fellowship are two of the blessings God desires for all His children.

As Paul's hearers strove to enter into this, they would feel the need of a deeper insight into their real oneness with Christ. They thereupon would learn to appreciate the truth that they had been crucified with Christ, that their "old man" had been crucified, and that they had died to sin in Christ's death and were living to God in His life. They would learn to know what it meant that the crucified Christ lived in them, and that they had crucified the flesh with its affections and lusts. It was because the crucified Jesus lived in them that they could live crucified to the world.

And so they would gradually enter more deeply into the meaning and the power of their high calling to live as those who were dead to sin and the world and self. Each in his own measure would bear about in his life the marks of the cross, with its sentence of death on the flesh, with its hating of the self-life and its entire denial of self. There would be growing conformity in them to their crucified Redeemer in His deep humility and entire surrender of His will to the life of God.

It is no easy school and no hurried learning—this school of the cross. But it will lead to a deeper understanding and a higher appreciation of the redemption of the cross, through the personal experience of the *fellowship* of the cross.

Crucified with Christ

*I have been crucified with Christ; it is no
longer I who live, but Christ lives in me.*

Galatians 2:20

THE thought of fellowship with Christ in His bearing the cross has often led to the vain attempt in our own power to follow Him and bear His image. But this is impossible for man until he first learns to know something of what it means to say, "I have been crucified with Christ."

Let us try to understand this. When Adam died, all his descendants died with him and in him. In his sin in Paradise, and in the spiritual death into which he fell, I had a share: I died in *him*. And the power of that sin and death, in which all his descendants share, works in every child of Adam every day.

Christ came as the second Adam. In His death on the cross all who believe in *Him* had a share. Each one may say in truth, "I have been crucified with Christ. As the representative of His people, He took them up with Him on the cross, *and me too*." The life that He gives is the crucified life, in which He entered heaven and was exalted to the throne, standing as a Lamb who had been slain (see Rev. 5:12). The power of His death and life work in me, and as I hold fast the truth that I have been crucified with Him, and that now I myself live no more but *Christ* lives in me, I receive power to conquer sin. The life that I have received from Him is a life that has been crucified and made free from the power of sin.

We have here a deep and very precious truth. Most Christians have but little knowledge of it. That knowledge is not gained easily or speedily. It requires a great longing indeed to be dead to all sin. It calls for a strong faith, wrought by the Holy Spirit, so that the union with Christ crucified—the fellowship of His cross—can day by day become our life. Truly the life that He lives in heaven has its strength and its glory in the fact that it is a *crucified* life. And the life that He imparts to the believing disciple is likewise a *crucified* life with its victory over sin and its power of access into God's presence.

It is definitely true that I no longer live, but Christ lives in me as the Crucified One. As faith realizes and holds fast the fact that the crucified Christ lives in me, life in the fellowship of the cross becomes a possibility and a blessed experience.

Crucified to the World

*But God forbid that I should boast except in the
cross of our Lord Jesus Christ, by whom the world
has been crucified to me, and I to the world.*

Galatians 6:14

WHAT Paul had written in Galatians 2 is here in
the end of the epistle confirmed and expressed
still more strongly. He speaks of his only glory being
that *in Christ* he has indeed been crucified to the world
and entirely delivered from its power. When he said "I
have been crucified with Christ," it was not only an inner spiritual truth, but an actual, practical experience
in relation to the world and its temptations. Christ had
spoken about the world hating Him, and His having
overcome the world. Paul knows that the world which
nailed Christ to the cross had in that deed done the same
to *him*. He boasts that he lives as one *crucified* to the
world, and that now the world as an impotent enemy
was crucified to *him*. It was this that made him glory in
the cross of Christ: It had produced a complete deliverance from the world.

How very different the relation of Christians to the
world in our day! They agree that they may not commit
the sins that the world allows. But except for that they are
good friends with the world, and have liberty to enjoy as
much of it as they can if they keep from open sin. They

do not know that the most dangerous source of sin is the love of the world with its lusts and pleasures.

O Christian, when the world crucified Christ, it crucified you *with* Him, When Christ overcame the world on the cross, He made you an overcomer *too*. He calls you now, at whatever cost of self-denial, to regard the world, in its hostility to God and His kingdom, as a crucified enemy over whom the cross can ever keep you conqueror.

What a different relationship to the pleasures and attractions of the world the Christian has who by the Holy Spirit has learned to say: "I have been crucified with Christ; . . . [the crucified] Christ lives in me!" (Gal. 2:20). Let us ask God fervently that the Holy Spirit, through whom Christ offered Himself on the cross, may reveal to us in power what it means to "boast . . . in the cross of our Lord Jesus Christ, by whom the world has been crucified to me" (6:14).

The Flesh Crucified

*Those who are Christ's have crucified
the flesh with its passions and desires.*

Galatians 5:24

OF the flesh Paul teaches us, "In me (that is, *in
my flesh*) *nothing good dwells*" (Rom. 7:18). And
again, "The carnal mind is *enmity against God*; for it is
not subject to the law of God, *nor indeed can be*" (8:7).
When Adam lost the spirit of God, he became flesh.
Flesh is the expression for the evil, corrupt nature that
we inherit from Adam. Of this flesh it is written, "Our
old man was crucified with Him" (6:6). And Paul puts
it here even more strongly: "Those who are Christ's have
crucified the flesh."

When the disciples heard and obeyed the call of
Jesus to follow Him, they honestly meant to do so; but
as He later on taught them what that would imply, they
were far from being ready to yield immediate obedience.
And similarly, those who are Christ's and have accepted
Him as the Crucified One often little understand what
that includes. By that act of surrender they actually have
crucified the flesh and consented to regard it as an *accursed* thing, nailed to the cross of Christ.

Alas, how many there are who have never for a
moment thought of such a thing! It may be that the
preaching of Christ crucified has been defective. It may
be that the truth of our being crucified *with* Christ has

never been taught! These novices shrink back from the self-denial that it implies; and as a result, where the flesh is allowed in any measure to have its way, the Spirit of Christ cannot exert His power.

Paul taught the Galatians: "Walk in the Spirit, and you shall not fulfill the lust of the flesh" (Gal. 5:16). "As many as are led by the Spirit of God, these are sons of God" (Rom. 8:14). And only as the flesh is kept in the place of crucifixion can the Spirit guide us in living faith and fellowship with Christ Jesus.

Blessed Lord, how little I understood when I accepted You in faith that I crucified once for all the flesh with its passions and lusts! I beseech You humbly, teach me so to believe and so to live in You, the Crucified One, that with Paul I may ever boast in the cross on which the world and the flesh are crucified.

Bearing the Cross

He who does not take his cross and follow after Me is not worthy of Me. . . . He who loses his life for My sake will find it.
Matthew 10:38–39

WE have looked at some of Paul's great words to the Galatians about the cross and our being crucified with Christ. Let us now turn to the Master Himself to hear what He has to teach us. We shall find that what Paul could teach openly and fully after the crucifixion was already stated by the Master—in words that could at first hardly be understood, but which contained the seed of the full truth.

It was in the ordination charge, when Christ sent forth His disciples, that He first used the expression that the disciple must take up his cross and follow Him.

The only meaning the disciples could attach to these words was from what they had often seen: An evildoer who had been sentenced to death by the cross was led out bearing his cross to the place of execution. In bearing the cross, he acknowledged the sentence of death that was on him. And Christ wanted His disciples to understand that their nature was so evil and corrupt that it was only in losing their natural life that they could find the true life. Of Himself it was true that *all* His life He bore His cross—the sentence of death that He knew to rest upon Him on account of our sins. And so He would have each disciple bear his personal cross—the sentence of death upon himself and his evil, carnal nature.

The disciples could not at once understand all this. But Christ gave them seed words, which would germinate in their hearts and later on begin to reveal their full meaning. The disciple was not only to carry the sentence of death in himself, but was also to learn that in following the Master to His cross he too would find the power to lose his life—and to receive, instead of it, the life that would come through the cross of Christ.

Christ asks of His disciples that they should forsake all and take up their cross—give up their whole will and life—and follow Him. The call comes to us, too, to give up the self-life with its self-pleasing and self-exaltation, and bear the cross in fellowship with Him—and so shall we be made partakers of His victory.

Self-Denial

Then Jesus said to His disciples, "If anyone desires to come after Me, let him deny himself, and take up his cross, and follow Me."

Matthew 16:24

CHRIST had for the first time definitely announced that He would have to suffer much and be killed and be raised again. Peter rebuked Him, saying, "Far be it from You, Lord; this shall not happen to You!" (16:22). Christ's answer was, "Get behind Me, Satan!" (16:23). The spirit of Peter, seeking to turn Christ away from the cross and its suffering, was nothing but Satan tempting Him to turn aside from the path which God had appointed as our way of salvation.

Christ then adds the words of our text, in which He uses for the second time the words "take up the cross." But with that He uses a most significant expression revealing what is implied in the cross: "If anyone desires to come after Me, *let him deny himself*, and take up his cross." When Adam sinned, he fell out of the life of heaven and of God into the life of the world and of self. Self-pleasing, self-sufficiency, self-exaltation—this became the law of his life. When Jesus Christ came to restore man to his original place, "being in the form of God, . . . *[He] made Himself of no reputation*, taking the form of a bondservant . . . and . . . *humbled himself* . . . even [to] the death of the cross"

(Phil. 2:6–8). What He has done Himself He asks of all who desire to follow Him: "If anyone desires to come after Me, let him deny himself."

Instead of denying himself, Peter denied his Lord: "I do not know the Man!" (Matt. 26:74). When a man learns to obey Christ's commands, he says of *himself*: "I do not know the man." The secret of true discipleship is to bear the cross, to acknowledge the death sentence that has been passed on self, and to deny any right that self has to rule over us.

Death to self is to be the Christian's watchword. The surrender to Christ is to be so entire, the surrender for Christ's sake to live for those around us so complete, that self is never allowed to come down from the cross to which it has been crucified but is ever kept in the place of death.

Let us listen to the voice of Jesus: "Deny self." And let us ask that, by the grace of the Holy Spirit, as the disciples of a Christ who denied Himself for us, we may ever live as those in whom self has been crucified with Christ and in whom the crucified Christ now lives as Lord and Master.

He Cannot Be My Disciple

If anyone comes to Me and does not hate . . .
his own life . . . he cannot be my disciple. *And*
whoever does not bear his cross and come after Me
cannot be my disciple. . . . *Whoever of you does*
not forsake all that he has cannot be my disciple.

Luke 14:26–33

FOR the third time Christ speaks about bearing the cross. He gives new meaning to it when He says that a man must hate his own life and forsake all that he has. Thrice over He solemnly repeats the words that without this a man *cannot* be His disciple.

"If anyone . . . does not hate . . . his own life." And why does Christ make such an exacting demand the condition of discipleship? Because the sinful nature we have inherited from Adam is indeed so vile and full of sin that, if our eyes were only opened to see it in its true state, we would flee from it as loathsome and incurably evil. "The carnal mind is enmity against God" (Rom. 8:7); the soul that seeks to love God cannot but hate the "old man" which is corrupt through its whole being. Nothing less than this, the hating of our own life, will make us willing to bear the cross and carry within us the sentence of death on our evil nature. It is not till we hate this life with a deadly hatred that we will be ready to give up the old nature to die the death that is its due.

Christ has one word more: "Whoever . . . does not forsake all that he has," whether in property or character, "cannot be My disciple." Christ claims all. Christ undertakes to satisfy every need and to give a hundredfold more than we give up. It is when by faith we become conscious of what it means to know Christ, and to love Him and to receive from Him what can in very deed enrich and satisfy our immortal spirits, that we shall count the surrender of what at first appeared so difficult, our highest privilege. As we learn what it means that *Christ is our life*, we shall "count all things loss for the excellence of the knowledge of Christ Jesus [our] Lord" (Phil. 3:8). In the path of following Him, and ever learning to know and to love Him better, we shall willingly sacrifice *all*, self with its life, to make room for Him who is *more* than all.

Follow Me

Then Jesus, looking at him, loved him, and said to him,
"One thing you lack: Go your way, sell whatever you
have, . . . and come, take up the cross, and follow Me."

Mark 10:21

WHEN Christ spoke these words to the young
ruler, he went away grieved. Jesus said: "How
hard it is for those who have riches to enter the kingdom
of God!" (10:23). The disciples were astonished at His
words. When Christ then declared that it was "easier for
a camel to go through the eye of a needle than for a rich
man to enter the kingdom of God," they were astonished
out of measure: "Who then can be saved?" Jesus replied,
"With men it is impossible, but not with God; for with
God all things are possible" (10:25–27).

To the rich young ruler Christ set forth the human
side of discipleship, the bearing of the cross. To His disciples, however, He reveals the divine side: God is able
to give men the will and the power to sacrifice all that if
they might enter the kingdom. He said to Peter, when he
had confessed Him as Christ, the Son of God, that flesh
and blood had not revealed it unto him but His Father
in heaven—to remind him and the other disciples that
it was only by divine teaching that they could make the
confession. So here, following this conversation with the
young ruler, He unveils the great mystery that it is only
by divine power that a man can take up his cross, can

lose his life, can deny himself and hate the life to which he is by nature so attached.

What multitudes have sought to follow Christ and obey His injunction and have found that they have utterly failed! What multitudes also have felt that Christ's claims were beyond their reach and have sought to be Christians without any attempt at the wholehearted devotion and the entire self-denial which Christ asks for!

Let us in our study of what the fellowship of the cross means take today's lesson to heart and believe that it is only by putting our trust in the living God, and in the mighty power with which He is willing to work in the heart, that we can attempt to be disciples who forsake all and follow Christ in the fellowship of His cross.

A Grain of Wheat

*Most assuredly, I say to you, unless a grain of wheat falls
into the ground and dies, it remains alone; but if it dies, it
produces much grain. He who loves his life will lose it, and he
who hates his life in this world will keep it for eternal life.*

John 12:24–25

ALL nature is a parable of how the losing of a life
can be the way of securing a truer and higher life.
Every grain of wheat, every seed throughout the world,
teaches the lesson that through death lies the path to
beautiful and fruitful life.

It was so with the Son of God. He had to pass
through death in all its bitterness and suffering before He
could rise to heaven and impart His life to His redeemed
people. And here, under the shadow of the approaching
cross, He calls His disciples: "If anyone serves Me, let
him follow Me" (12:26). He says to them: "He who hates
his life in this world will keep it for eternal life" (12:25).

One might have thought that Christ did not need to
lose His holy life before He could find it again. But so it
was: God had laid upon Him the iniquity of us all (see
Isa. 53:6) and He yielded to the inexorable law: through
death to life and to fruit.

How much more ought we, in the consciousness
of that evil nature and that death which we inherited in
Adam, be most grateful that there is a way open to us
by which, in the fellowship of Christ and His cross, we

can die to this accursed self! With what willingness and gratitude ought we to listen to the call to bear our cross, to yield our "old man" as crucified with Christ daily to that death which he deserves! Surely the thought that the power of the eternal Life is working in us ought to make us willing and glad to die the death that brings us into the fellowship and the power of life in a risen Christ.

Alas, how little this is understood! Let us believe that what is impossible to man is possible to God. Let us believe that the law of the Spirit of Christ Jesus, the risen Lord, can in very deed make His death and His life the daily experience of our souls.

Your Will Be Done

*O My Father, if it is possible, let this cup pass
from Me; nevertheless, not as I will, but as You will.*

Matthew 26:39

THE death of Christ on the cross is the highest and the holiest act that can be known by man outside the glory of heaven. And the highest and the holiest experience that the Holy Spirit can produce in us on earth is to keep us in daily fellowship with the cross of Christ. We need to enter deeply into the truth that Christ, the beloved Son of the Father, could not return to the glory of heaven until He had first given Himself over unto death. As this great truth opens up to us, it will help us to understand how, in our life and particularly in our fellowship with Christ, it is impossible for us to grow without surrendering ourselves every day to die to sin and the world, and so to abide in this unbroken fellowship with our crucified Lord.

And it is from Christ alone that we can learn what it means to have fellowship with His sufferings and to be made conformable unto His death. When, in the agony of Gethsemane, He looked forward to what that death on the cross would be, He had such a vision of what it meant to suffer the accursed death under the power of sin—with God's countenance so turned from Him that not a single ray of its light could penetrate the darkness —that He prayed that the cup might pass from Him.

But when no answer came, and He understood that the Father could not allow the cup to pass by, He yielded up His whole will and life in the words, "Your will be done." O Christian, through submission like your Lord's in His time of agony, you can enter into deeper fellowship with Him. In His strength your heart will be made strong to believe most confidently that God, in His omnipotence, will enable you to yield up your selfish desires, because you have in very fact been crucified with Him.

"Your will be done"—let this be the deepest and the highest attitude in your life. In the power of Christ with whom you have been crucified, and in the power of His Spirit, this definite, daily surrender to the ever-blessed will of God will become the joy and the strength of your life.

The Love of the Cross

*Then Jesus said, "Father, forgive them,
for they do not know what they do."*

Luke 23:34

THE seven words on the cross reveal not only the mind of Christ but also the dispositions that mark His disciples. Take the first three words, all of them expressions of His wonderful love.

"Father, forgive them, for they do not know what they do." He prays for His enemies. In the hour of their triumph over Him, and amidst the shame and suffering which they delight in showering on Him, He pours out His love in *prayer* for them. The call to everyone who believes in a crucified Christ is to go and do likewise— even as He has said, "Love your enemies, bless those who curse you, do good to those who hate you, and pray for those who spitefully use you and persecute you" (Matt. 5:44). The law of the Master is the law for the disciple: the love of the crucified Jesus, the only rule for those who believe in Him.

"Woman, behold your son! . . . Behold your mother!" (John 19:26–27). The love that cared for His enemies cared also for His friends. Jesus felt what the anguish must be in the heart of His widowed mother and He commits her to the care of the beloved disciple. He knew, also, that for John there could be no higher privilege and no more blessed service than that of taking *His* place in the care of Mary. Similarly, we who are the disciples of Christ must prove our love to Christ and to all who belong to Him by seeing to it that every lonely and needy one is comforted, and that every loving heart has some work to do in caring for those who belong to the blessed Master.

"Assuredly, I say to you, today you will be with Me in Paradise" (Luke 23:43). The penitent thief had appealed to Christ's mercy to remember him. With what readiness of joy and love Christ gives an immediate answer to his prayer!

Whether it was the love that prays for His enemies, or the love that cares for His friends, or the love that rejoices over the penitent sinner who was being cast out by man—in *all* Christ proves that His cross is a cross of love. The Crucified One is the embodiment of a love that passes knowledge.

With every thought of what we owe to that love, with every act of faith in which we rejoice in its redemption, let us prove that the mind of the crucified Christ is *our* mind, and that His love is not only what we trust in for ourselves, but also what guides us in our loving interaction with the world around us.

The Sacrifice of the Cross

*My God, My God, why have You forsaken
Me? . . . I thirst! . . . It is finished!*

Matthew 27:46; John 19:28, 30

THE first three words on the cross reveal love in its
outflow to men. The next three reveal love in the
tremendous *sacrifice* that it brought, necessary to deliver
us from our sins and give the victory over every foe. They
reveal the very mind that was in Christ and that also is
to be in us as the disposition of *our* whole life.

"My God, My God, why have You forsaken Me?"
How deep must have been the darkness that overshad-
owed Him, for not one ray of light could pierce it and He
could not utter "My Father"! It was this awful desertion—
breaking in upon that life of childlike fellowship with the
Father in which He had always walked—that caused Him
the agony and the bloody sweat in Gethsemane. "O My
Father . . . let this cup pass from Me" (Matt. 26:39)—but
it might not be, and He bowed His head in submission:
"Your will be done" (26:42). It was His love to God and
love to man—this yielding Himself to the very uttermost.
As we learn to believe and to worship that love, we too
shall learn to say: "Abba, Father, . . . not what I will, but
what You will" (Mark 14:36).

"I thirst." The body now gives expression to the terrible experience of what it passed through when the fire
of God's wrath against sin came upon Christ in the hour

of His desertion. He had spoken of "a certain rich man" crying, "I am tormented in this flame" (Luke 16:24). Christ utters His complaint of what He now suffered. Physicians tell us that in crucifixion the whole body is in agony with a terrible fever and pain. Our Lord endured it all and cried: "I thirst." Soul and body was the sacrifice He brought the Father.

And then comes the great word: "It is finished!" All that there was to suffer and endure had been brought as a willing sacrifice; He had finished the work the Father gave Him to do. His love held nothing back. He gave Himself to be an offering and a sacrifice. Such was the mind of Christ, and such must be the disposition of everyone who owes himself and his life to that sacrifice. The mind that was in Christ must be in us, ready to say: "My food is to do the will of Him who sent Me, and to finish His work" (John 4:34). May no day pass without our confidence growing fuller in Christ's finished work and our heart more entirely yielding itself like Him, a whole burnt offering in the service of God and His love.

The Death of the Cross

"Father, into Your hands I commit My spirit."
Having said this, He breathed His last.

Luke 23:46

LIKE David (see Ps. 31:5), Christ had often commit-ted His spirit into the hands of His Father for His daily life and need. But here is something new and very special. He gives up His spirit into the power of death, gives up all control over it, to sink down into the darkness and death of the grave, where He can neither think nor pray nor will. He surrenders Himself to the utmost into the Father's hands, trusting Him to care for Him in the dark and, in due time, to raise Him up again.

If we have indeed died in Christ and now, in faith, are every day to carry about with us the death of our Lord Jesus, this word is the very one that we need. Just think once again what Christ meant when He said that we must hate and lose our life.

We died in Adam; the life we receive from him is death; there is nothing good or heavenly in us by nature. It is to this inward evil nature, to all the life that we have from this world, that we must die. There cannot be any thought of any real holiness without totally dying to this self or "old man." Many deceive themselves because they seek to be alive in God before they are dead to their own nature—a thing as impossible as it is for a grain of wheat to be truly alive before it dies. This total dying to self lies at the root of all true piety. The spiritual life must grow out of death!

And if we ask how we can do this, we find the answer in the mind in which Christ died. Like Him, we cast ourselves upon God without knowing how the new life is to be attained; but as we in fellowship with Jesus say, "Father, into Your hands I commit my spirit," and depend simply and absolutely upon God to raise us up into the new life, there will be fulfilled in us the wonderful promise of God's Word concerning the exceeding greatness of His power in us who believe, according to the mighty power which He wrought in Christ when He raised Him from the dead.

This indeed is the true test of faith—a faith that lives every day and every hour in absolute dependence upon the continual and immediate quickening of the divine life in us by God Himself through the Holy Spirit.

It Is Finished

When Jesus had received the sour wine,
He said, "It is finished!"

John 19:30

THE seven words of our Lord on the cross reveal to us His mind and disposition. At the beginning of His ministry He said, "My food is to do the will of Him who sent Me, and to *finish His work*" (4:34). In all things, the small as well as the great, His aim was to accomplish God's work. In the High Priestly Prayer at the end of the three years' ministry, He could say, "I have glorified You on the earth. *I have finished the work* which You have given Me to do" (17:4). He sacrificed all, and in dying on the cross could in truth say: "It is finished."

With that word to the Father He laid down His life. With that word He was strengthened, after the terrible agony on the cross, in the knowledge that all was now fulfilled. And with that word He uttered the truth of the gospel of our redemption, that all that was needed for man's salvation had been accomplished on the cross.

This disposition should characterize every follower of Christ. The mind that was in Him must be in us—it must be our food, the strength of our life, *to do the will of God in all things and to finish His work*. There may be small things about which we are not conscientious, and so we bring harm to ourselves and to God's work. Or we draw back before some great thing which demands too much sacrifice. In every case, we can find strength to perform our duty in Christ's word "It is finished." His finished work secured the victory over every foe. By faith we may appropriate that dying word of Christ on the cross and find the power for daily living and dying in the fellowship of the crucified Christ.

Child of God, study the inexhaustible treasure contained in this word: "It is finished." Faith in what Christ accomplished on the cross will enable you to manifest in daily life the spirit of the cross.

The Righteousness of God

*Abraham believed God, and it was
accounted to him for righteousness.*

Romans 4:3

He believed . . . God, who gives life to the dead.

Romans 4:17

LET us now, after listening to the words of our Lord Jesus about our fellowship with Him in the cross, turn to St. Paul, and see how through the Holy Spirit he gives the deeper insight into what our death in Christ means.

You know how the first section of Romans is devoted to the doctrine of justification by faith in Christ. After speaking of the awful sin of the heathen (see 1:18–32) and then of the sin of the Jew (see 2:1–29), he points out how both Jew and Gentile are "guilty before God" (3:19). "All have sinned and fall short" (3:23). And then he sets forth the free grace by which we are given the redemption that is in Christ Jesus (see 3:21–31). In chapter 4, he points to Abraham as having, when he believed, understood that God justified him freely by His grace, and not for anything that he had done.

Abraham had not only believed this but something more. "He believed . . . God, who gives life to the dead and calls those things which do not exist as though they did" (4:17). The two expressions are most significant, as indicating the two essential elements there are in the redemption of man by Christ Jesus. There is the need of justification by faith, to restore man to the favor of God. But this is not all; more is needed. He must also be given a new life. Just as justification is by faith alone, so is regeneration also. Christ died because of our sins; He was raised to secure our justification and that He might send the Holy Spirit to effect our regeneration and sanctification.

In the first section (down to Romans 5:11) Paul deals exclusively with the great thought of our justification. But in the second section (5:12–8:39) he expounds that wonderful union with Christ by which, through faith, we died with Him, by which we live in Him, and by which, through the Holy Spirit, we are made free, not only from the punishment but also from the power of sin, and are enabled to live a life of righteousness, of obedience, and of sanctification.

Dead to Sin

How shall we who died to sin live any longer in it?

Romans 6:2

AFTER having, in the first section of the epistle to the Romans (1:16–5:11), expounded the great doctrine of *justification* by faith, Paul proceeds, in the second section (5:12–8:39), to unfold the related doctrine of the *new life* by faith in Christ. Taking Adam as a figure of Christ, he teaches that just as we all really and actually died in Adam, so that his death reigns in our nature, even so, in Christ, those who believe in Him actually and effectually died to sin, were set free from it, and became partakers of the new holy life of Christ.

He asks the question: "How shall we who died to sin live any longer in it?" In these words we have the deep spiritual truth that our death to sin in Christ delivers us from its power, so that we no longer may or need to live in it. The secret of true and full holiness is by faith, and thus, in the power of the Holy Spirit, to live in the consciousness that I am dead to sin.

In expounding this truth he reminds them that they were baptized *into the death of Christ*. We were buried with Him through baptism into death. We became *united with Him* by the likeness of His death. Our "old man" was crucified with Him, that the body of sin might be done away—rendered void and powerless. Take time and quietly, asking for the teaching of the Holy Spirit, ponder these words until the truth masters you: I am indeed dead to sin in Christ Jesus. As we grow in the consciousness of our union with the crucified Christ, we shall experience that the power of His life in us has made us free from the power of sin.

Romans 6 is one of the most blessed portions of the New Testament of our Lord Jesus, teaching us that our "old man," the old nature that is in us, was actually crucified with Him, so that now we need no longer be in bondage to sin. But remember, it is only as the Holy Spirit makes Christ's death a reality within us that we shall know, not by force of argument or conviction, but in the reality of the power of a divine life, that we are in very deed dead to sin. The sole requirement for this blessed life of victory is a continual living *in* Christ Jesus—in the power of His resurrection.

Dead with Christ

*If we died with Christ, we believe
that we shall also live with Him.*

Romans 6:8

THE reason that God's children live so little in the power of the resurrection life of Christ is because they have so little understanding of or faith in their death with Christ. How clearly this appears from what Paul says: "If we died with Christ, we believe that we shall also live with Him"; it is the knowledge and experience that gives us the assurance of the power of His resurrection in us. "[Christ] died to sin once for all; but the life that He lives, He lives to God" (6:10). It is only because and as we know that we are dead with Him that we can live with Him.

On the strength of this, Paul now appeals to his readers: "Likewise you also, reckon yourselves to be dead indeed to sin, but alive to God in Christ Jesus our Lord" (6:11). The words "Likewise . . . reckon yourselves" are a call to an act of bold and confident faith. Reckon yourselves to be indeed dead to sin, as much as Christ is, and alive to God in Christ Jesus. This appeal gives us divine assurance of what we actually are and have in Christ. And this comes not as a truth that our minds can somehow master and appropriate but as a reality which the Holy Spirit will reveal within us. In

His power we accept our death with Christ on the cross as the power of our daily life.

Then we are able to accept and obey the command: "Do not let sin reign in your mortal body, . . . but present yourselves to God as being alive from the dead. . . . For sin shall not have dominion over you" (Rom 6:12–14). "Having been set free from sin, you became slaves of righteousness. . . . Present your members as slaves of righteousness for holiness" (6:18–19). "Now having been set free from sin . . . you have your fruit to holiness" (6:22).

The whole chapter of Romans 6 is a revealing answer to its opening question: "How shall we *who died to sin* live any longer in it?" (6:2). Everything depends upon our acceptance of this divine assurance: If we died with Christ, as He died, then, because He now lives with God, we have the assurance that *in Him* we have the power to live pleasing unto God.

Dead to the Law

*You also have become dead to the law through the body
of Christ. . . . Having died to what we were held by,
so that we should serve in the newness of the Spirit.*

Romans 7:4, 6

THE believer is not only dead to *sin* but also dead
to the *law*. This is a deeper truth, giving us deliverance from the thought of a life of effort and failure, as
it opens the way to a life lived in the power of the Holy
Spirit. "You shall" is done away with; the power of the
Spirit takes its place.

In the remainder of this seventh chapter of Romans
(7:7–24), we have a description of the Christian as he still
tries to obey the law—but utterly fails. He experiences
that "in [him] (that is, in [his] flesh) nothing good dwells"
(7:18). He finds that the law of sin, notwithstanding
his utmost efforts, continually brings him into captivity
and ultimately wrings from him the cry: "O wretched
man that I am! Who will deliver me from this body of
death?" (7:24).

In the whole passage, the man of action is everywhere
"I," without any thought of the Spirit's help. It is only
when he has given utterance to his cry of despair that
he is brought to see that he is no longer under the law
but under the rule of the Holy Spirit. "There is therefore
now no condemnation" (such as he had experienced in
his attempt to obey the law) "to those who are in Christ

Jesus. . . . For the law of the Spirit of life in Christ Jesus has made me free from the law of sin and death" (Rom. 8:1–2).

As chapter 7 gives us the experience that leads to being a captive under the power of sin, chapter 8 reveals the experience in the life of a man *in* Christ Jesus, who has now been made free from the law of sin and death. In the former, we have the life of the ordinary Christian doing his utmost to keep the commandments of the law and to walk in God's ways, but ever finding how much there is of failure and shortcoming. In the latter, we have the man who knows that he is *in Christ Jesus*, dead to sin and alive to God—who by the Spirit has been made free and is kept free from the bondage of sin and of death.

Oh that Christians understood what the deep meaning is of Romans 7, where a man learns that in him (that is in his fleshly nature) there is no good thing, and that there is no deliverance from this state except by yielding to the power of the Spirit, making him free from the power and bondage of the flesh and so fulfilling the righteousness of the law in the power of the life of Christ!

The Flesh Condemned on the Cross

*For what the law could not do in that it was weak through
the flesh, God did by sending His own Son in the likeness of
sinful flesh, on account of sin: He condemned sin in the flesh.*

Romans 8:3

IN Romans 8:7 Paul writes: "The carnal mind is enmity
against God; for it is not subject to the law of God,
nor indeed can be." Here Paul enlarges upon the depth
of sin that there is in the flesh. In chapter 7 he had said
that in the flesh there is no good thing. Here he goes
deeper, and tells us that the carnal mind is enmity against
God: It hates God and His law. It was on this account
that God condemned sin in the flesh on the cross; all the
curse that was placed upon sin was placed upon the flesh
in which sin dwells. It is as the believer understands this
that he will cease from any attempt at seeking to perfect
in the flesh what is begun in the Spirit. The two are set
in deadly, irreconcilable antagonism.

See how this lies at the very root of the true Christian
life: "[God] condemned sin in the flesh, that the righteous
requirement of the law might be fulfilled in us who do
not walk according to the flesh but according to the
Spirit" (8:3–4). All the requirements of God's law will
be fulfilled, not in those who strive to keep and fulfill
that law—a thing that is utterly impossible—but in those
who walk by the Spirit and, in His power, live out the

life that Christ won for us on the cross and imparted to us in the resurrection.

Oh that God's redeemed children might learn the double lesson. In me (that is, in my flesh, in the old nature which I have from Adam), there dwells literally no good thing that can satisfy the eye of a holy God! And that flesh can never by any process of discipline, or struggling, or prayer, be made better than it is! But the Son of God in the likeness of sinful flesh—in the form of a man—condemned sin on the cross. "There is therefore now no condemnation to those who are in Christ Jesus, who do not walk acccording to the flesh, but acccording to the Spirit" (Rom. 8:1).

Jesus Christ and Him Crucified

I determined not to know anything among you except Jesus Christ and Him crucified. And my speech and my preaching were . . . in demonstration of the Spirit and of power.

First Corinthians 2:2, 4

THIS text is very often understood as setting forth Paul's purpose in his preaching: to know nothing but Jesus Christ and Him crucified. But it contains a far deeper thought. He speaks of his purpose not only with regard to the matter of his preaching but also as it affects his whole spirit and life—that in everything he seeks to act in conformity to the crucified Christ. Thus he writes, "[Christ] was crucified in weakness, yet He lives by the power of God. For we also are weak in Him, but we shall live with Him by the power of God toward you" (2 Cor. 13:4). Paul's whole ministry and manner of life bore the mark of Christ's likeness—crucified in weakness, yet living by the power of God.

Just before the words of our text Paul had written: "The message of the cross is foolishness to those who are perishing, but to us who are being saved it is the power of God . . . and the wisdom of God" (1 Cor. 1:18, 24). It was not only in his preaching but also in his whole disposition and deportment that he sought to act in harmony with that weakness in which Christ was crucified. He had so identified himself with the weakness of the cross, and its shame, that in his whole life and conduct he gave evidence that in everything he desired to show forth the likeness and the spirit of the crucified Jesus. Hence he says: "I was with you in weakness, in fear, and in much trembling" (1 Cor. 2:3).

It is on this account that he spoke so strongly: "Christ did not send me to baptize, but to preach the gospel, not with wisdom of words, lest the cross of Christ should be made of no effect" (1:17). "My preaching [was] not with persuasive words of human wisdom, but in demonstration of the Spirit and of power" (2:4). Have we not here the great reason why the power of God is so little manifested in the preaching of the gospel? Christ the crucified may be the subject of the preaching and yet there may be such confidence in human learning and eloquence that there is nothing to be seen of that likeness of the crucified Jesus which alone gives preaching its supernatural, its divine power.

May God help us to understand how the life of every minister and of every believer must bear the hallmark, the stamp of the sanctuary: Nothing but Jesus Christ, and Him crucified.

Temperance in All Things

Everyone who competes for the prize is temperate in all things. . . . I discipline my body and bring it into subjection.

First Corinthians 9:25, 27

PAUL here reminds us of the well-known principle that anyone competing for a prize in the public games is "temperate in all things." Everything, however attractive, that might be a hindrance in the race is given up or set aside. And this in order to obtain an earthly prize. And shall we, who strive for an incorruptible crown, and that Christ may be Lord of all—shall we not be temperate in all things that could in the very least prevent our following the Lord Jesus with an undivided heart?

Paul says: "I discipline my body and bring it into subjection." He would allow nothing to hinder him. He tells us: "One thing I do, . . . I press toward the goal for the prize" (Phil. 3:13–14). No self-pleasing in eating and drinking, no comfort or ease, would for a moment keep him from showing the spirit of the cross in his daily life or from sacrificing all, like his Master. Read the following four passages which comprise his life history: First Corinthians 4:11–13; Second Corinthians 4:8–12; 6:3–10; 11:23–28. The cross was not only the theme of his preaching but also the rule of his life in all its details.

We need to implore God that this disposition may be found in all Christians and preachers of the gospel, through the power of the Holy Spirit. When the death of Christ works with power in the preacher, then Christ's life will be known among the people. Let us pray that the fellowship of the cross may regain its old place, and that God's children may obey the injunction: "Let this mind be in you which was also in Christ Jesus" (Phil. 2:5). He humbled Himself and became obedient unto the death of the cross. And we must also. For, "if we have been united together in the likeness of His death, certainly we also shall be in the likeness of His resurrection" (Rom. 6:5).

The Dying of the Lord Jesus

Always carrying about in the body the dying of the Lord Jesus, that the life of Jesus also may be manifested in our body. . . . So then death is working in us, but life in you.

Second Corinthians 4:10, 12

PAUL here is very bold in speaking of the intimate union that there was between Christ living in him and the life he lived in the flesh, with all its suffering. He had spoken (see Gal. 2:20) of his being crucified with Christ, and Christ living in him. Here he tells how he was always bearing about in the body the dying of Jesus; it was through that that the life also of Jesus was manifested in his body. And he says that it was because the *death* of Christ was thus working in and through *him* that Christ's *life* could work in *them*.

We often speak of our abiding in Christ. But we forget that that means abiding in a *crucified* Christ. Many believers appear to think that when once they have claimed Christ's death in the fellowship of the cross, and have counted themselves as crucified with Him, that they may now consider it as past and done with. They do not understand that it is in the crucified Christ, and in the fellowship of His death, that they are to abide *daily* and *unceasingly*. The fellowship of the cross is to be the life of a daily experience. The self-emptying of our Lord, His taking the form of a servant, His humbling Himself and becoming obedient unto death, even the death of the cross—this mind that was in Christ is to be the disposition that marks our *daily* life.

"Always carrying about in the body the dying of the Lord Jesus." This is what we are called to as much as was Paul. If we are indeed to live for the welfare of men around us, if we are to sacrifice our ease and pleasure to win souls for our Lord, it must be true of us, as of Paul, that we are able to say: Death works in us, but life in those for whom we pray and labor. For it is in our fellowship in the *sufferings* of Christ that the crucified Lord can live out and work out His life in us and through us.

Let us learn the lesson that the abiding in Christ Jesus for which we have so often prayed and striven is nothing less than the abiding of the *Crucified One* in us and we in Him.

The Cross and the Spirit

How much more shall the blood of Christ, who
through the eternal Spirit offered Himself without
spot to God, cleanse your conscience?

Hebrews 9:14

THE cross is Christ's highest glory. The glory which
He received from the Father was entirely owing to
His having humbled Himself to the death of the cross.
"Therefore God also has highly exalted Him" (Phil. 2:9).
The greatest work which the Holy Spirit could ever do
in the Son of God was when He enabled Him to yield
Himself as a sacrifice and an offering for a sweet-smelling
savor. And the Holy Spirit can now do nothing greater or
more glorious for us than to lead us into the fellowship
and likeness of that crucified life of our Lord.

Have we not here the reason that our prayers for
the mighty working of the Holy Spirit are not more
abundantly answered? We have prayed too little that the
Holy Spirit might glorify Christ in us in the fellowship
and the conformity to His *sufferings.* The Spirit, who led
Christ to the cross, is longing and is able to maintain in
us the life of abiding in the crucified Jesus.

The Spirit and the cross are inseparable. The Spirit
led Christ to the cross; the cross brought Christ to the
throne to receive the fullness of the Spirit to impart to
His people. The Spirit taught Peter at once to preach
Christ crucified; it was through that preaching that the

three thousand received the Spirit. In the preaching of the gospel, in the Christian life, as in Christ, so in us: The Spirit and the cross are inseparable. It is the sad lack of this mind and disposition of the crucified Christ— sacrificing self and giving up the world to win life for the dying—that is a major cause of the feebleness of the church. Let us beseech God fervently to teach us to say: We have been crucified with Christ; in Him we have died to sin; we are "always carrying about in the body the dying of the Lord Jesus" (2 Cor. 4:10). So shall we be prepared for that fullness of the Spirit which the Father longs to bestow.

The Veil of the Flesh

*Therefore, brethren, having boldness to enter the Holiest by
the blood of Jesus, by a new and living way which He
consecrated for us, through the veil, that is, His flesh.*

Hebrews 10:19–20

IN the temple there was a veil between the Holy Place
and the Most Holy. At the altar in the court the blood
of the sacrifice was sprinkled for forgiveness of sins. That
gave the priest entrance into the Holy Place to offer God
the incense as part of a holy worship. But into the Most
Holy Place, behind the veil, the high priest alone might
enter once a year. That veil was a symbol of Christ's body;
even though believing Jews could receive forgiveness of
sin, until it was rent full access and fellowship with God
was impossible.

When Christ died, the veil was rent. Christ dedicated
a new and living way to God by means of the rent veil
of His flesh. This new way, by which we now can enter
into the Most Holy Place—the place of fellowship with
God—ever passes through the rent veil of the flesh.
Every believer has potentially "crucified the flesh with
its passions and desires" (Gal. 5:24). Every step on the
new and living way for entering into God's holy presence
maintains the fellowship with the cross of Christ. For the
rent veil of the flesh has reference not only to Christ and
His personal sufferings but also to our experience in the
likeness of His sufferings.

Have we not here the reason why many Christians can never attain to close fellowship with God? They have never yielded the flesh as an accursed thing to the condemnation of the cross. They desire to enter into the blessedness offered by their Lord, and yet they allow the flesh with its desires and pleasures to rule over them. God grant that we may rightly understand, in the power of the Holy Spirit, that Christ has called us to hate our life, to lose our life, to be dead with Him to sin that we may live to God with Him. There is no way to a full, abiding fellowship with God but through the rent veil of the flesh, through a life with the flesh crucified in Christ Jesus. God be praised that the Holy Spirit ever dwells in us to keep the flesh in its place of crucifixion and condemnation, and to give us the abiding victory over all temptations!

Looking unto Jesus

*Let us run with endurance the race that is set before
us, looking unto Jesus, the author and finisher of
our faith, who for the joy that was set before
Him endured the cross, despising the shame.*

Hebrews 12:1–2

IN running a race the eye and heart are ever set upon
the goal and the prize. The Christian is here called to
keep his eye fixed on Jesus enduring the cross, as the one
object of imitation and desire. In our whole life we are
ever to be animated by His Spirit as He bore the cross.
This was the way that led to the throne and the glory of
God. This is the new and living way which He opened
for us through the veil of the flesh. It is as we study and
realize that it was because of His bearing the cross that
God so highly exalted Him, that we shall then walk in
His footsteps—bearing our cross after Him, with the
flesh condemned and crucified.

The impotence of the church is greatly owing to the
fact that this cross-bearing attitude of Jesus is so little
preached and practiced. Most Christians think that as
long as they do not commit actual sin they are at liberty
to possess and enjoy as much of the world as they please.
There is so little insight into the deep truth that the world,
and the flesh that loves the world, is hostile to God. The
result is that many Christians seek and pray for years for
conformity to the image of Jesus, and yet fail so entirely.

They do not know—they do not seek with the whole heart to know—what it is to die to self and the world.

It was for the joy set before Him that Christ endured the cross—the joy of pleasing and glorifying the Father, the joy of loving and winning souls to Himself. We have indeed need of a new crusade with the proclamation: This is the will of God, that as Christ found His highest happiness *through His endurance of the cross*, and received thereby from the Father the fullness of the Spirit to pour down on His people, so it is only in *our fellowship of the cross* that we can really become conformed to the image of God's Son. Believers, awake to this blessed truth and run the race, ever looking to the crucified Jesus! You will receive power to win for Christ the souls He has purchased on the cross.

Outside the Gate

The bodies of those animals, whose blood is brought into the sanctuary . . . are burned outside the camp. Therefore Jesus also, that He might sanctify the people with His own blood, suffered outside the gate. Therefore let us go forth to Him, outside the camp, bearing His reproach.

Hebrews 13:11–13

THE blood of the annual sin offering was brought into the Most Holy Place; the body of the sacrifice was burned outside the camp (see Lev. 16:27–28). Even so with Christ. His blood was presented to the Father; but His body was cast out as an accursed thing, outside the camp.

And so we read in Hebrews 10: "[Let us] enter the Holiest by the blood of Jesus" (10:19). And in our text: "Let us go forth to Him, outside the camp, bearing His reproach." The deeper my insight is into the boldness which His blood gives me in God's presence, so much greater will be the joy with which I enter the inner sanctuary. And the deeper my insight is into the shame of the cross which He bore on my behalf outside the camp, the more willing shall I be, in the fellowship of His cross, to follow Him outside the camp, bearing His reproach.

There are many Christians who love to hear of the boldness with which we can enter into the Most Holy Place through Christ's blood who yet have little desire for the fellowship of His reproach and are unwilling to separate themselves from the world with the same boldness with which they think to enter the sanctuary. The Christian suffers inconceivable loss when he thinks of entering into the Most Holy Place in faith and prayer, and then feels himself free to enjoy the friendship of the world so long as he does nothing actually sinful. But the Word of God has said: "Do you not know that friendship with the world is enmity with God?" (James 4:4); "Do not love the world or the things in the world. If anyone loves the world, the love of the Father is not in him" (1 John 2:15); "Do not be conformed to this world" (Rom 12:2).

To be a follower of Christ implies a heart given up to testify for Christ in the midst of the world, if by any means some may be won. To be a follower of Christ means to be like Him in His love of the cross and His willingness to sacrifice self that the Father may be glorified and that men may be saved.

Blessed Savior, teach me what it means that I am called to follow You outside the camp, bearing Your reproach, and so to bear witness to Your holy redeeming love, as it embraces the men who are in the world—to win them back to the Father. Blessed Lord, let the spirit and the love that was in You be in me too, that I may at any cost seek to win the souls for whom You have died.

Alive for Righteousness

*Who Himself bore our sins in His own body on the tree,
that we, having died to sins, might live for righteousness.*

First Peter 2:24

HERE we have in the epistle of Peter the same lessons that Paul has taught us. First, *the atonement of the cross*: "Who Himself bore our sins in His own body on the tree." And then, *the fellowship of the cross*: "That we, having died to sins, might live for righteousness."

In this last expression we have the great thought that a Christian cannot live for righteousness except as he knows that he has died to sin. We need the Holy Spirit to make our death to sin in Christ such a reality that we know ourselves to be forever free from its power and so yield our members to God as instruments of righteousness. The words give us a short summary of the blessed teaching of Romans 6.

Dear Christian, it cost Christ much to bear the cross and then to yield Himself for it to bear Him. It cost Him much when He cried: "Now My soul is troubled, and what shall I say? 'Father, save Me from this hour'? But for this purpose I came to this hour" (John 12:27).

Let us not imagine that the fellowship of the cross, of which Peter speaks here—"that we, having died to sins, might live for righteousness"—is easily understood or experienced. It connotes that the Holy Spirit will teach us what it is to be identified with Christ in His cross. It requires that we realize by faith how actually we shared with Christ in His death, and now, as He lives in us, that we abide in unceasing fellowship with Him, the Crucified One. This costs self-sacrifice; it costs earnest prayer; it costs a wholehearted surrender to God and His will and the cross of Jesus; it costs abiding in Christ and unceasing fellowship with Him.

Blessed Lord, make known to us day by day through the Holy Spirit the secret of our life in You: "We in You and You in us." Let Your Spirit reveal to us that, as truly as we died in You, You now live in us the life that was crucified and now is glorified in heaven. Let Your Spirit burn the words deep into our hearts. Having died unto sin and being forever set free from its dominion, let us know that sin can no more reign over us or have dominion. Let us in the power of Your redemption yield ourselves unto God as those who are alive from the dead, ready and prepared for all His will.

Followers of the Cross

By this we know love, because He laid down His life for us.
And we also ought to lay down our lives for the brethren.

First John 3:16

G REATER love has no one than this, than to lay
down one's life for his friends" (John 15:13). Here
our Lord reveals to us the inconceivable love that moved
Him to die for us. And now, under the influence and in
the power of that love dwelling in us, comes the message: "*We also ought to lay down our lives for the brethren.*"
Nothing less is expected of us than a Christlike life and
a Christlike love, proving itself in all our dealings with
our brethren.

The cross of Christ is the measure by which we know
how much Christ loves us. That cross is the measure,
too, of the love which we owe to the brethren around
us. It is only as the love of Christ on the cross possesses
our heart and daily animates our whole being that we
personally shall be able to love the brethren. Our secret
fellowship in the cross of Christ is to manifest itself in
our sacrifice of love not only to Christ Himself but also
to all who belong to Him.

The life to which John calls us here is something
entirely supernatural and divine. It is only the faith of
Christ Himself living in us that can enable us to accept
this great command in the assurance that Christ Himself
will work it out in us. It is He Himself who calls to each

of us: "If anyone desires to come after Me, let him deny himself, and take up his cross, and follow Me" (Matt. 16:24). Nothing less than this, a dying to our own nature, a faith that our "old man," our flesh, has been crucified with Christ, so that we no longer need to sin—nothing less than this can enable us to say: I love His commandments; this commandment, too, is not grievous.

But for such fellowship and conformity to the death of Christ, nothing will avail but the daily, unbroken abiding in Christ Jesus which He has promised us. By the Holy Spirit revealing and glorifying Christ in us, we may each trust Christ Himself to live out His life in us. He who proved His love on the cross of Calvary—He Himself, He alone—can enable us to say *in truth*: He laid down His life for me; I ought to lay down my life for the brethren.

It is only as the great truth of the indwelling Christ obtains a place in the faith of the church which it has not now that the Christlike love to the brethren will become the mark of true Christianity—a token by which all men shall know that we are Christ's disciples. This is what will bring the world to believe that God has loved us even as He loved Christ.

Following the Lamb

These are the ones who follow the Lamb wherever He goes.
Revelation 14:4

IT may not be easy to say exactly what is implied in this "following of the Lamb" in the heavenly vision. But of this we can be sure, that whatever it is in glory will be the counterpart of what it is to follow in the footsteps of the Lamb here upon earth. As the Lamb's actions and character on earth revealed what the Lamb in heaven would be like, so His followers on earth can show forth something of the glory of what it is to follow Him in heaven.

And how may the footsteps of the Lamb be known? "He humbled Himself" (Phil. 2:8); "He was led as a lamb to the slaughter, . . . so He opened not His mouth" (Isa. 53:7). It is the meekness and gentleness and humility that marked Him which calls for His followers to walk in His footsteps.

Our Lord Himself said: "Learn from Me, for I am gentle and lowly in heart, and you will find rest for your souls" (Matt. 11:29). Paul writes: "Let this mind be in you which was also in Christ Jesus" (Phil. 2:5). And then he teaches us what that mind consisted of: "Being in the form of God . . . [He] made Himself of no reputation, taking the form of a bondservant. . . . He humbled Himself and became obedient to the point of death, even the death of the cross" (Phil. 2:6–8). The Lamb is our Lord and Lawgiver. He opened the only path that leads to the throne of God. It is as we learn from Him what it means to be gentle and lowly, what it means to empty ourselves, to choose the place of the servant, to humble ourselves and become obedient, even unto death, the death of the cross, that we shall find the new and living way that leads us through the rent veil into the Holy of Holies.

"Therefore God also has highly exalted Him and given Him the name which is above every name" (2:9). It is because Christians so little bear the mark of this self-emptying and humiliation even unto death that the world refuses to believe in the possibility of a Christ-filled life.

Children of God, oh come and study the Lamb who is to be your model and your Savior. Let Paul's words be the keynote of your life: "I have been crucified with Christ; it is no longer I who live, but Christ lives in me" (Gal. 2:20). Here you have the way to follow the Lamb even to the glory of the throne of God in heaven.

To Him Be the Glory

*To Him who loved us and washed us from our
sins in His own blood, and has made us kings
and priests to His God and Father, to Him be
glory and dominion forever and ever. Amen.*

Revelation 1:5–6

SOME of my readers may feel that it is not easy to
understand the lesson of the cross and to carry it out
in their lives. But do not think of it as a heavy burden
or yoke that you have to bear. Christ says: "My yoke is
easy and My burden is light" (Matt. 11:30). *Love makes
everything easy.* Do not think of your love to Him but,
rather, of His great love to *you*, given through the Holy
Spirit! Meditate on this day and night, until you have absolute assurance: He loves me unspeakably. It is through
the love of Christ on the cross that reluctant souls like
ours are drawn to Him.

Here also we discover the answer as to what will enable us to desire and love the fellowship of the crucified
Jesus: nothing less than His love poured out through the
continual breathing of the Holy Spirit into our heart.

"*To Him who loved us*"—Be still, O my soul, and
think what this everlasting love is that seeks to take possession of you and fill you with joy unspeakable.

"*And washed us from our sins in His own blood*"—Is
that not proof enough that He will never reject me; that

I am precious in His sight, and through the power of His blood am well-pleasing to God?

"*And has made us kings and priests to His God and Father*"—And He now preserves us by His power, and will strengthen us through His Spirit to reign as kings over sin and the world and to appear as priests before God in intercession for others. O Christian, learn this wonderful song and repeat it until your heart is filled with love and joy and courage, and day by day turns to Him in glad surrender: "*To Him be glory and dominion for ever and ever. Amen.*"

Yes, to *Him*, who has loved me, and washed me from my sins in His blood, and made me a king and a priest—*to Him be the glory in all ages*. Amen.

The Blessing of the Cross

*But God forbid that I should boast except in the
cross of our Lord Jesus Christ, by whom the world
has been crucified to me, and I to the world.*

Galatians 6:14

ONE of the blessings of the cross consists in this,
that it teaches us to know the worthlessness of
our efforts and the utter corruption of our own nature.
The cross does not offer to improve human nature or to
supplement what man is able to do. Many people, indeed,
use it in this way, like patching a new cloth on an old
garment; but this rends the garment, and such persons
walk about in torn clothes. They go from one minister
to another without finding what they seek. No, the old
garment, our old man, must be laid aside and given over
to the death of the cross. For the cross causes all that is
of the lost nature of man to die the accursed death, and
the "I" is revealed as a malefactor. The cross breaks the
staff over all that is of the old nature.

Whosoever has been brought to the cross through
the Spirit has learned to pronounce the death sentence
on his old nature—has broken the staff over himself; for
whatever does not bear the mark of the cross lies under
the curse. He who would save his life remains under the
curse. If we have learned through the Spirit to understand
the cross, then we have lost our life and will no longer

expect any good from our old nature; nor will we judge others, but ourselves only.

But as long as we have not been taught this lesson through the Spirit, we shall try to find good in ourselves—something of worth in God's sight, and upon which the sentence of death need not be passed. And if we find nothing good at all, we easily fall into a false grief which the Evil One eagerly uses to make us despair, by saying: "You may as well give up. God will not trouble about you. There is nothing for you but failure."

But this is not what God desires. What we possess by nature must be nailed to the cross and we must put on the new man. The cross brings man to utter bankruptcy of himself, and then God can come to our aid. The cross brought the disciples of Jesus once to such an end of themselves, a condition which even the words of the Master had failed to do. It took from them the aureole of holiness which they thought they had won in the three years that they followed Jesus and it taught them to know themselves. And so they were prepared to receive the Holy Spirit, who would impart a new nature and a new life. For we cannot separate the cross from the Spirit. *We can have no Easter and no Pentecost until we have first had a Good Friday.*

Through *the cross alone* are we prepared for life in the fullness of God; only he who is crucified with Christ can be a vessel unto honor.

Our "old man" must be crucified with Christ (see Rom. 6:6), and in the resurrection of Christ we will find the roots of our new life (see 1 Pet. 1:3). Whosoever loses his life shall find it. We must learn the lesson of the cross as condemned and rejected ones who have been crucified with Christ. Then the door will be open for a life of power and blessing. All that belongs to death must be given over to death, even as the body is laid away in the earth because it belongs to the earth.

The Holy Spirit, the Eternal Spirit, is unchangeable. He brought Christ, our Head, to the cross, and us His children with Him. For this work in us is twofold. On the one hand it leads us to death and all that belongs to death; and on the other hand, to that life which God has placed within us and which leads from glory to glory!

TRANSLATED FROM
IN THE FOOTPRINTS OF THE LAMB
BY G. STEINBERGER

Prayer

How I praise You, O my God, for the gift of the Holy Spirit, who will reveal to me the secret of the cross of Christ! The Spirit strengthened Christ to offer Himself to God on the cross. The cross gave Christ the right to receive the fullness of the Spirit from the Father to pour out on all flesh. The cross gives us the right to receive the Spirit. And the Spirit teaches us to love the cross, and to partake of the life crucified with Christ.

O my Father, I thank You that You give the immediate, continual working of the Spirit in my heart, so that the crucified Christ may be formed within me and His life maintained within me.

Father, I beseech You humbly, teach me and Your people so to know this work of the Spirit, and to yield ourselves to Him to take full possession of us, that the crucified Lord Jesus may be glorified in us.

AMEN.

PUBLICATIONS

Fort Washington, PA 19034

This book is published by CLC Publications, an outreach of CLC Ministries International. The purpose of CLC is to make evangelical Christian literature available to all nations so that people may come to faith and maturity in the Lord Jesus Christ. We hope this book has been life changing and has enriched your walk with God through the work of the Holy Spirit. If you would like to know more about CLC, we invite you to visit our website:

www.clcusa.org

To know more about the remarkable story of the founding of CLC International we encourage you to read

LEAP OF FAITH

Norman Grubb

Paperback
Size 5¹/₄ x 8, Pages 248
ISBN: 978-0-87508-650-7
ISBN (e-book): 978-1-61958-055-8